Lord, I Believe But Help Me With My Unbelief

BRENDA SUMMERVILLE

Love Clones Publishing
www.lcpublishing.net

Lord, I Believe But Help My Unbelief
Copyright @ 2015 by Brenda Summerville

Scripture taken from the New International Version®. Copyright © 2005 by Zondervan. Used by permission. All rights reserved.

ISBN: 978-0692375068

Love Clones Publishing
Dallas, TX
www.lcpublishing.net

DEDICATION

This book is dedicated to an awesome bunch of siblings, my brother BJ and my sister Gail. Thank you for introducing me to the joys and magic of reading! To the Tate Brothers, Larenz, Larron and Lahmard for planting the seed of curiosity, encouragement and hope. I picked up a pen and the rest is history. I am forever grateful!

THANK YOU

First off to my Lord Jesus. My number one supporter! Thank you for providing direction, support, wisdom and love. Thank you for holding me down since the very beginning. I am yours forever! Thank you to my publisher Love Clones Publishing for your patience, support and bomb cover! Thank you to the Rev. Dr. Charles G. Adams for setting the mood for my story. Thank you to iT Girl Forever and the iT Factor Agency. Your press is awesome! You're a rockstar! Thank you to family and friends who offered prayers and encouragement. Remember to speak the things that be not as though they were! Believe, hope, trust and especially love! Until next time, Brenda.

TABLE OF CONTENTS

FOREWORD

Matthew 17:19-20, "Then came the disciples to Jesus apart, and said, "Why could not we cast him out?" And Jesus said unto them, "Because of your unbelief: for verily I say unto you, if ye have faith as a grain of a mustard seed, ye shall say unto this mountain, Remove hence to yonder place; and it shall remove: and nothing shall be impossible unto you."

These words of Jesus Christ are directed to each and every one of you. All are included. None is excluded. Jesus says, "If you have faith, astonishing things, miraculous things, amazing things will happen." These words are addressed to you, "If you have faith." These words were first spoken by Jesus to another group, to the disciples, after their embarrassing failure to heal the epileptic son of a troubled and solicitous father. Though Jesus had already given them power to do it, and had commissioned them to use their power, they were unable to bring about the healing.

So, after Jesus had healed the young man instantly, the disciples took Jesus aside out of the glare of the crowd so they could get a private lesson in healing. They said to Jesus, "Why couldn't we do what you did?" Jesus answered, "Because of your unbelief: for truly I tell you, if you have faith as a grain of mustard seed, you shall say unto this mountain, 'move hence to yonder place', and it will move, and nothing will be impossible for you."

Nothing is possible without faith. Nothing is impossible with faith. Actually, we live by faith and cannot live without faith. Some people have erroneously staged a conflict between faith and reason; but if you think about it, reason is based on faith. Others have tried to start a fight between faith and work; but if you just think about it, you will realize that faith without work is dead. Anything you do, anywhere you go depends on your faith.

By faith every farmer sows his seed. Every manufacturer produces the goods. Every merchant stocks the shelves. Every banker loans the cash. Every diner eats what comes out of the kitchen that he or she has not inspected. You really don't know what you're eating. You're eating by faith, or you're not eating at all.

By faith the scientist goes to the laboratory believing that there will be a discovery of truth. By faith the surgeon picks up the scalpel. By faith the lawyer stands before the bar, and by faith the child of God stretches out on the word of God.

So Jesus is saying to his disciples, ancient and current, "What is it that you want to be? What is it that you want to achieve? I can hear them telling Jesus what they wanted to do but had not done. What is it that you want to achieve? I can hear your answer even though your tongues are silent. I can hear your minds clicking. Somebody is saying, "I want a praying spirit." Somebody is saying, "I want a closer walk with God." Somebody is saying, "I want more power with God in prayer. Somebody is saying, "I want a clear conscience." Somebody is saying, "I want a pure heart."

- "I want a healthier, slimmer, stronger body."
- "I want to be strong enough to handle stress."
- "I want to be able to stand calmly and serenely under fire."

9

- "I want to have more knowledge of the Bible."
- "I want to love and serve humanity."
- "I want to do more for my Church and my Christ."
- "I want to live in happiness and peace at home."
- "I want to be a better spouse."
- "I want to be a better son or daughter."
- "I want to be a better parent."
- "I want to be a better person."
- "I want to acquire the true values of life."
- "I want more patience."
- "I want more peace."
- "I want more faithfulness."
- "I want more love."
- "I want more life."
- "I want more discipline."
- "I want more security."
- "I want less anxiety."
- "I want more will power."
- "I want everything good in life that life can afford for anybody." And
- "I want, when I get through living, to die easy when I die and shout salvation as I fly away to be at rest."

What do I want?

What do you want?

And why have we not yet achieved it? Perceived it?

Received it?

Jesus says, "Because you haven't believed it."

"Because of your unbelief." "For if you have faith, you shall have made yourself an open channel through which the power of God can flow and work and bless. And when the power of God flows through you,

- Your mountains will be moved.
- Your obstacles will be overcome.
- Your troubles will be transformed into triumphs.
- Your sickness will be sanctified into strength.
- Your hearts will be purified.
- Your minds will be purged of poisonous assumptions and presumptions of inferiority.
- Your bodies will be strengthened.
- Your talents will be developed.
- Your homes will be established.
- Your churches will be built.
- Your joy will be full.
- Humanity will be blessed.
- The world will be saved.
- The community will be fortified, and
- God will be glorified, if you have faith!

Without faith, you are all stopped up, stymied and stagnant on the brink of opportunity. Without faith, your holy ghost breathing system is jammed, clogged, blocked, stopped up, and the power just can't get through. When the power can't get through, the lights cannot come on, the generators cannot be started. It takes power to do anything, and in order to get power, you've got to keep your holy ghost channels open so that you can receive the power from God.

The late Dr. Zodie Johnson, of blessed memory, took me on a tour of the schools over which she was the Area Superintendent in Detroit Michigan. She took me to a primary school class where the little students were learning how to help, in case they ever were confronted, with a cardio-pulmonary emergency. The instructor was teaching them how to intervene in behalf of sudden victims of cardiac arrest. The children were learning that the first thing the rescuer must do is to raise the head of the victim. You have to raise the neck off the floor so that the air passages can be open and clear to receive the oxygen. Then the breath-bearing O^2 that comes from mouth to mouth resuscitation can enter into the respiratory channels of the victim from the lungs of the rescuer.

It won't be long before the victim can start breathing on his own. But, if the neck of the victim is left down, the passageways will not clear; they will be clogged and constricted, and no matter how long or how hard you breathe into the mouth of the victim, the air will never reach the lungs because the passageway is not clear. So it is with us: we too have been stricken with the cardiac arrest of tragedy in our lives, and we are all victims.....

- Victims of foolishness.
- Victims of faithlessness.
- Victims of stress in life.
- Victims of trouble on every hand.
- Victims of mountainous oppressions.
- Victims of military madness.
- Victims of a materialism gone rampant.
- Victims of a poisoned environment.
- Victims of manifold frustrations.
- Victims of perplexities and complexities that we cannot understand.
- Victims of sins that we have committed against us.
- Victims of satanic influences.
- Victims of diabolical schemes.
- Victims of lies we can't stop, tragedies we can't prevent, calamities we can't avoid, and

injustices we can't correct.

We need air. We need power. We need enablement. We need the ability to achieve our purposes, and to reach our goals, and to do our work, and to make some progress; but the Rescuer can't do us any good if the Holy Ghost air passages in us are clogged and jammed shut against the breath of God. You can sit up in church, stand up in the choir, be up in the pulpit; but it won't help you unless you are open and receptive to receive from God the breath you need. Faith is your appropriation and appreciation of the strength of God that is already available here and now.

What kind of students are kept in Kindergarten all day? The brightest and the best? Not at all. They selected the lowest achievers that they could find; they got the least likely to succeed. They targeted the students who seemed to be at that early age unteachable, uneducable, retarded, deficient -- low achievers. The slow learners were the very ones who were chosen to stay in kindergarten all day. The lowest achieving, least likely students, poorest students, most deprived students were being taught all day how to read, how to do arithmetic. They taught them how to speak French and Spanish. I was amazed when I visited that kindergarten and saw those little children reading with comprehension, speaking French, speaking Spanish and speaking English, not Ebonics. I wanted to know, "How did these miracles happen?"

The answer was:
- "Somebody believed in these children.
- Somebody had faith in these children.
- Somebody thought that these children could learn if they were taught."

Aren't you glad somebody believed in you enough to teach you something and bring the best out of you? Aren't you glad somebody believed in you and taught you how to believe in yourself? Well, your kindergarten teacher is no longer around to do it for you. Now you've got to do it for yourself.

If you have faith, you can do great things. If you have faith, you can be elevated from a low achiever to a high achiever.

If you have faith, you can do anything wonderful you want to do.

So, you ought to step out of church, face a brand new year, resolved in your heart and mind that you're going to believe in God, in people and in yourself. For if You believe in God, if You believe in others and if You believe in You, You can do anything you want to do. You can be anything you want to be. You can rise as high as you reach. You can achieve anything you believe. You can have anything you claim, because your Savior and my Savior is blessing us right now, breathing the Holy Ghost into us right now.

Everybody has at least two minds. Whenever you want to do anything, there are always two minds speaking to you. One mind is the mind of faith. The other mind is the mind of doubt. The mind of faith speaks in the still, small voice of a mustard seed. The mind of doubt speaks in the loud, boasting voice of a mountain. The mountain stands for doubt. The mustard seed stands for faith.

- Faith says, "Greatness will inhabit smallness."
- Doubt says, "Greatness will crush smallness."

- Faith says, "There is enough power in you to move mountains."
- Doubt says, "Mountains are impregnable and immovable."
- Faith says, "All things are possible."
- Doubt says, "Negatives forces are in charge of the universe."
- Faith says, "You can do all things through Christ."
- Doubt says, "You can do nothing but fail."
- Faith says, "Walk on by me."
- Doubt says, "Fall flat on your face."
- Faith says, "Victory will be yours."
- Doubt says, "You are already defeated."
- Faith says, "Attempt great things for God."
- Doubt says, "Don't even try it."
- Faith says, "You shall overcome."
- Doubt says, "You shall be overcome."
- Faith says, "Fight on."
- Doubt says, "Surrender without a struggle."
- Faith says, "Keep it up."
- Doubt says, "Give it up."
- Faith says, "Fear nothing."
- Doubt says, "Fear everything."

But, now show me one thing that doubt ever accomplished.
- Show me one river that doubt ever crossed.
- Show me one bridge that doubt ever swung through space.

- Show me one book that doubt ever wrote or read.
- Show me one tree that doubt ever planted.
- Show me one cause that doubt ever advanced.
- Show me one good mission that doubt ever sustained.
- Show me one soul that doubt ever saved.
- Show me one life that doubt ever improved.
- Show me one sickness that doubt ever healed.
- Show me one church that doubt ever built.
- Show me one business that doubt ever established.
- Show me one world that doubt ever redeemed.
- Show me one child that doubt ever reared.
- Show me one person that doubt ever empowered.

The answer is, there's not one. No not one.

But let me show you what faith has done and what faith can still do!
By faith, Booker T. Washington founded Tuskegee Institute.
By faith, W.E.B. DuBois organized the NAACP.
By faith, Mordecai Johnson saved Howard University.
By faith, Benjamin Elijah Mays developed Morehouse College.
By faith, Marion Anderson sang her way from rejection because of color to acclamation because of her character and charisma.
By faith, Jesse Owens lectured to Hitler with his feet.
By faith, Joe Louis became a world champion.

By faith, Jackie Robinson broke the color bar in
baseball.
By faith, Thurgood Marshall desegregated American
education.
By faith, Martin Luther King Jr. declared a dream to
the World.
By faith, Nelson Mandela stepped up from prisoner to
president of South Africa.
By faith, the Berlin Wall came tumbling down in 1989.
By faith, two million Black men marched on
Washington, D.C. in 1995.
By faith,

- Enoch walked with God.
- Abraham looked for a city.
- Jacob wrestled with the angel.
- Moses walked through the Red Sea.
- Joshua conquered Jericho.
- Sampson defeated the Philistines.
- David slew Goliath.
- Solomon built a temple.
- Elijah prayed down fire from heaven.
- Elisha raised a dead child.
- Ezekiel raised up dry bones in the valley.
- Daniel went to sleep in the Lion's Den.

By faith, the three Hebrew children kissed away the
flames in the fiery furnace.
By faith, Jesus died on Calvary.
By faith, Jesus was raised from the dead,
Drew the sting out of death.

Snatched the victory from the grave.
By faith, Paul preached the gospel in Rome.
By faith, John saw the Holy City.
By faith, You will move mountains, open up rivers.
  You shall overcome.
  You shall run through troops.
  You shall leap over walls.
  You shall do great things.
  You shall receive power from God.
By faith, Nothing,
  Nothing,
  Nothing,
  Nothing,
  Nothing will be impossible for you!

If you have faith, you will change history into hope, you will transform tragedy into triumph, you will change adversity into advancement. Only if you have faith!

"If You Have Faith"
By Charles G. Adams
Pastor
Hartford Memorial Baptist Church
Detroit Michigan

My Disclaimer:

"When I came to you, sisters and brothers, I did not come with eloquence or superior wisdom as I proclaimed to you the testimony about God. For I resolved to know nothing while I was with you except Jesus Christ and him crucified. I came to you in weakness and fear, and with much trembling. My message and my preaching were not with wise and persuasive words, but with a demonstration of the Spirit's power, so that your faith might not rest on men's wisdom, but on God's power." (1 Corinthians 2:1-5 NIV)

Confessions are good for the soul

"All art is a kind of confession, more or less oblique. All artist, if they are to survive, are forced, at last, to tell the whole story: to vomit the anguish up." James Baldwin

There are two things I can't stand. Compromise and Contradiction. First contradiction. If I say something, I mean it. I don't want to change my mind or go against what I believe. I want to do what I say and say what I mean. It's that simple. Second compromise- I don't want to settle for less or let alone nothing. I don't want to miss out and I don't want to fail. I don't want to sell my soul and lose my spirit. I don't want to compromise my morals for money. I don't want crumbs or the leftovers. It's that simple. Over the past seven years I did a turn around, I have contradicted myself and I have compromise my life. I didn't want to do that. I fought it tooth and nail. But I lost to a higher power who is GOD!

I once was in a loving relationship with God but one day something dramatic happen. I turned my back on my wonderful relationship and in the process I lost my mind! I decided that I wanted to take control

22

and I took the wheel! It took me seven years to find myself and in the process I found my way back to God. I was finally welcome back into my loving relationship and this is my story...

My story is very simple nothing new. It is about a battle, a struggle between God and me. Over the next chapters I will explain how you can compromise and contradict your life but for the greater good, God's sake. I battled depression and contemplated suicide. I was at my lowest and no one, but God brought me back! This book is my testimony of how I followed my own will and turned my back on God's will. I now understand that all of the discipline, all of the trials, pain and the pruning were all worth it so I could testify of God's goodness. I knew God but I didn't understand God. I believed God but I didn't trust God. I had my own expectations but God had a different expectancy of my life.

This is my confession, of my unbelief!

Chapter 1
Pretty on the Outside, Hurting on the Inside.

How are you doing? Do you really care? Can you see me? Do you hear me? I was drowning but no one saw me struggling.......... I am my sister's keeper, right? I am my sister... -Me

The winter of 1993 was a bittersweet season for me. My father died a few days after my birthday. My father, a man whom I didn't have a good relationship with and I didn't get an opportunity to make it any better.   I was barely passing in school and this was my final semester of college. I had just gotten audited from the IRS and I was being sexually harassed and discriminated against by one of my professors. The best part of 1993 was that I had won a scholarship for women from a major automotive manufacturer. I was very proud of that award. It was one accomplishment that brought a glimmer of light in my life. I was a poor, struggling young black woman from the west side of Chicago and this was my first major accomplishment in the male dominated profession that I love. I was happy with myself but hurt by the drama that was around me. The drama called racism and white male privilege.

In May of that year I was so glad to be coming home to Chicago. College was hard! I know now that the reason things were so hard for me is because I didn't know God. Well let me rephrase that, I knew God, I was raised in the church but I didn't know God intimately. I did not know the intimacy and what God's true capabilities were. When I was very young I knew I was different and special. I knew that the Holy Spirit had touched my life. I knew that I had the gift of presence. I knew that I was spirit filled, but I was afraid to let my light shine. Marianne Williamson, explained it so beautifully, "It is not our darkness that we are afraid of it is our light." I have always been afraid of my light. I was always worried about what people would think and say of me. My power was dormant because of my fear. And because of that fear I was passive for so long. I became afraid of everything. In the result of that fear I lost my heart, my courage, my strength and myself. I just existed and I became a servant to things like my career, my money, clothes, shoes, handbags, jewelry, and my family and to people. When you're a servant of things and not a servant of the Lord, people will take advantage of you. I served everything but God. When I went through the IRS audit, my father dying and problems with school it took me to a level of rejection and failure that I had never experienced before in my life. I had no money, no help and no support. I didn't know how to handle those failures. I will never forget that day when I heard a voice telling me that I was a failure and to just kill myself because there was no way out. That was the lowest point of my life. It was rock bottom for me. And the sad thing is I entertained the idea of taking my life. This was my first nervous breakdown.

During the summer of 1993 I was interviewing constantly for jobs but had no offers. Despite no employment opportunities, I was still very much excited because this was a new beginning and a chance for me to build the life I wanted, make money, travel and see the world. In late July I interviewed with an automotive manufacturer that I was skeptical about working for, let's just say they were not my first choice. After about five interviews in different cities I finally received a call with an offer. I was under the impression that I would be relocating to Michigan but it was another Midwest City. I had no family or friends there. I didn't know anyone. Again fear sat in, it was the fear of the unknown. But deep down I could hear the Holy Spirit telling me that it was time to grow up. I left home scared and unsure of myself.

Now if you remember earlier I told you I was sexually harassed in college not for sex, but against my gender, I was discriminated against because of my race and my sex. I experienced double the hate because I am black and a woman. This trauma was still in my spirit. I had never allowed myself to heal because there was so much going on during my last semester of college. So I carried hurt, pain and anger. I woke up every morning and faced the world as a pretty girl, clothes are perfect, hair and nails done, but I was hurt and wounded on the inside. I sought help while in college but a few sessions don't heal. Healing is a process where in my case it took years to rehabilitate me. I had lost a big chunk of my self-esteem. I was perpetrating like I'm cool with myself but I wasn't. I arrived at my Corporate America job broken but functional, hurt but happy. I wasn't bringing my whole self to the table. I was not bringing my complete authentic self. I was a wounded warrior stepping into another battle. When you're not 100 percent healed it is only a setup for disaster.

CHAPTER 2
TELL OUR STORIES THE WAY WE EXPERIENCE OUR STORIES

Tell our stories the way we experience our stories
- Tananariva Due

No one speaks for me but me... -Me

I was out of the college environment but I stepped into the world of Corporate America. I felt as if I'd gotten out of the frying pan into the fire. The fire of Corporate America. When I arrived at my new job I was very eager to please my new boss. But it was the same old program with the same old white men and same old agenda. Everything about my new job was the same old thing. I was miserable and after praying, crying and more prayer the good Lord moved me to Michigan. I thought the move would be better for me emotionally because I was now up north with tons of opportunities for me to grow professionally. But it was only worst! Some of the people were unfriendly and some were miserable because they lacked the education to move forward with the company. Some folks resented my youth. Some resented the fact that I was a black woman and had a job. I encounter so many people who had no problem telling me that I am here due to affirmative action. Being black and a woman was something I was taught to celebrate not to be ashamed of it. I had a group of people that reminded me everyday that I crashed the party and was not invited! I made it to Detroit the Automotive Capital of the World and it was not what I thought. It was not what I dreamt it to be. There were no support or encouragement for me. I was on my own and I began to question my self-esteem and my worth. I started trying to get myself out of the situation. I begin posting for jobs just trying my best to get the hell out. Every time I tried to get into another department a door would just close in my face. You know the saying, for every step I take the Lord will take two? Well I was stepping but the Lord was standing still.

One night a feeling of despair overcame me I knew I was stuck in a job I did not love. I was stuck with people who hated my guts simply because I took advantage of the chance to better myself with an education. I was stuck with people who resented my skin color. I was overwhelmed by this newfound realization. My mind was racing and my second nervous breakdown came on and not at the best time. I was on the dance floor at a happy hour for the Black MBA. I started to cry uncontrollably and I could not breathe. I knew I was having a heart attack! I was angry with God; I was pissed off at God! The Detroit chapter of the Black MBA surrounded me and chucks of my self-esteem fell to the dance floor. I deemed myself a failure yet again.

My doctor called my illness a panic attack. I refuse to believe it because panic attack for me is synonymous with mental illness. I was ashamed and really did not know what to do or how to save myself. I recouped myself and gathered my composure and tried to go on with life but an air of sadness followed me.

I went back to my old habit of job posting but no leads came back. My friend started to notice my depression and she introduced me to some inspirational books. Three quotes that stands out from Florence Shovel Shinn's book, " The Collected Wisdom of Florence Shovel Shinn; The Game of Life and How to Play it: Your word is your wand, The secret door to success, The power of the spoken word" are, " behold, I set before thee the open door to destiny which no man nor woman can shut for it is nailed back. The second, 'promotion comes neither from the east nor the west, I am the judge I set one up and take one down'. The final, "there is no competition on the spiritual plane, what is rightly mine is given to me under grace'. I took these quotes, as my confirmation of God. God is telling me what, God can do but I was caught up in my own will. I believed it from God but I still had unbelief of God's power. I read and heard the words but I still felt the fear that I was stuck. I was constantly trying to be strong but I was failing. My health was deteriorating. I had developed ulcers, GERD (Gastroesophageal reflux disease), I had developed fibroids, my hair was falling out and my face was breaking out. I had gained over 50 pounds and I was completely out of control. I couldn't even control my dream. I was constantly having recurring dream that my managers would take turns combing my hair and as they combed my hair it would get healthier, stronger and longer. Very long! This dream continued for the next seven years! How in the hell do you have the same dream for seven years straight!

I had finally received a call back from another job for an interview. The interview was flawless and the hiring manager really liked me for the position. Then another blow, the hiring manager called me back and said that the Vice President's next-door neighbor was graduating from the University of Michigan and needed a job. This was my first taste of nepotism. I was hurt and livid! The white hiring manager had the nerve to tell me to my face that I should be happy that I was here and that I had a job. He told me that the neighbor's kid needed a position and I already had one so oh well. I was left like WTF?

This was devastating and a major turning point for me. I had never experienced a social injustice in this form before. I had experienced racism through words but never through actions. I have had people called me the N word to my face but I never had anything withheld or taken away because someone else comes along with no experience. All they have to offer is privilege and that privilege allows them to take my blessings. Then to have a person in power tell me that I should be grateful that I'm still at the party was hard words to swallow. I didn't leave the house for a month because I was embarrassed, scared, unsure, not trusting anyone, hurt, grieving, angry, sick, humiliated and very fearful.

My friends told me that I needed a mentor and that I should befriend the white men and let them help me but again I didn't want to compromise myself. I shouldn't have to. I have the degree and I have the experience. My race and gender has been compromised enough. Only God could understand my hurt and pain. I have experienced racism before but this was deep because white America was standing in the way of something I wanted. This was the first time I was told no to something that I thought I deserved. I didn't understand it and it was unfair. I didn't know how to handle it or how to recover from the rejection. All I knew was that this white man had blocked me from something I wanted very badly and I was now angry at the world. I had worked so hard to get to that point. I had persevered and I had sacrificed and now I was told that I should just be happy to be in but at the bottom. That statement for me felt like I'm not getting anywhere with this company and I simply lost all hope and I sank into darkness. I was struggling and no one heard my cry.

CHAPTER 3
LET ME INTRODUCE YOU TO AN OLD FRIEND

Write hard and clear about what hurts. - Ernest

Hemingway

Write to release the shame, the past and the defeat. I'm

writing as if my life depends on it and in reality it does...

-Me

In the spring of 1997 a college friend came to visit me. At this point in my life I was very sick and suffering from depression. My friend visit was very much welcome and appreciated. It was truly a gift from God!

My friend had bought her toddler daughter and this neat little pink bible with her. I was excited to see her child and to have a baby in my house was cool but it also reminded me of the fact that I might never be able to conceive because issues with my fibroids. The cute pink bible was called the Women Devotional Bible. At this point in my life I was not reading my bible at all. All I had in my home was the King James

Version and I couldn't understand it anyway so why bother? There were times I tried to read it. I would read the book of Psalms only to comfort me but King David's words brought no peace to my spirit and no comfort to my aching mind.

One night while my friend was in the shower and the baby was asleep. I can't remember if I knock over the bible or how exactly it fell over onto my bedroom floor. But it open up to James 1, 3-7. I read and though, maybe this could be for me. It read: *Because you know the testing of your faith develops perseverance. Perseverance must finish its work so that you may be mature and complete nothing lacking anything."* I love the word perseverance! I can get with the word because all of my life I had to persevere. I had to fight, I had to struggle, and I had to work harder and smarter. I was the girl that finished last but I finish! I knew how to be steadfast but I was so broken I just didn't want to be steadfast any longer.

After reading the words my heart had the desire but my mind was like no! My mind was mentally and emotionally burned out! But my heart felt the Holy Spirit and knew the Holy Spirit wanted me to read it.

I continue to read the entire chapter and the book of James. I was excited because I had a feeling that my prayers and pain was not falling on deaf ears.

The next morning we were up and out early to Sunday morning church service at Hartford Memorial Baptist church. I had told my friend about this pastor, The Rev. Doctor Charles Gilchrist Adams and the church. The members affectionally called Pastor Adams PA so of course I was a member and I called him PA as well. I was so excited. I was like the women at the well yall! I had encountered a man who sermons were words I never heard before! They were hopeful, soothing and empowering. He was beyond brilliant and welcome women into his pulpit. Women were in ministry roles and working hard in the church. I was amazed every Sunday! Going to Hartford was my boost to keep me going all week. It helps me maintain the little faith that I had in myself let alone in the world. Hartford church was my refuge and P.A's sermons were my comfort. They called the church progressive Baptist. Growing up my Baptist church was nothing like this. Women at Hartford were doing so much besides teaching Sunday school and frying the chicken.

The church was political, socially connected in the community, Detroit, Africa and the world! Charles Adams spoke with knowledge and authority. Outside of the Rev. Dr. Martin Luther King Jr. and Mayor Harold Washington I never heard black men speak like that. He was highly educated and I never experience that with Pastors. The pastors I knew were called and maybe had a few bible classes but they were not taught at the graduate or Ph.D. level. I like to joke and say I was experiencing the new math! But in reality I was. I was experiencing theology. Mathematics is a discipline. The types of problems it addresses, the method it uses to address the problems and the results it achieved define mathematics. Very much like theology. I was experiencing religion not as I learn it growing up but I was experiencing it through religious truths and different concepts of God.

God had not reveal it to me yet. I wasn't mature and complete yet! Like I said before healing is a process. I was experiencing the new math aka 'theology' but little did I know that years later of would be a part of it and using it to help and comfort others.

I was so happy to introduce my friend to my new church home and my friend was happy that I finally found solace. She was happy that on any given Sunday I found some peace for my reality. Reading James 1: 3-7 was a paradigm shift for me. Things begin to make sense and I started to hear and understand better. I was still in a job I hated but somehow things felt different. An old friend had returned.

CHAPTER 4
OVERCOMING MYSELF

"Courage is what it takes to stand up and speak: Courage is also what it takes to sit down and listen."

-Winston Churchill

"Don't get stuck in your own story."- Oprah Winfrey

My faith had completely diminished. I was running around on empty. P.A. sermons' kept me going but it wasn't enough. All of the sermons seemed to be on faith. I knew the word. I use to love that word. I heard it used by members of my family. I can remember have faith in yourself and God! My self worth was tapped out and I would tell you that God had abandoned me. The word I loved was not so lovable and it was now distant for me. I was lying to myself and to the church folks at Hartford because I knew my faith was not strong, hell it was damn near gone!

I was at church on Sunday and the sermon and scripture was on Hebrew chapter 12. Well we all know that Hebrew is the faith book! Hebrew 12,

Therefore, since we are surrounded by such a great cloud of witnesses, let us throw off everything that hinders and the sin that so easily entangles and let us run with perseverance the race marked out for us. Let us fix our eyes on Jesus the author and perfector of our faith, who for the joy set before him endured the cross, scorning its shame and sat down at the right hand of the throne of God. Consider him who endures such oppositions from sinful men, so that you will not grow wary and lose heart. In your struggle against sin you have not yet resisted to the point of shedding your blood. And you have forgotten that word of encouragement that addresses you as sons and daughters. Do not make light of the Lord's discipline and do not lose heart when he rebukes you because the Lord disciplines those God love and punishes everyone God accepts as children. Endure hardship as disciplines, God is treating you as a child."

Hearing Hebrew 12 it struck two cords, first the word perseverance is back and second it's not about me! I had to dig deep back into my childhood Sunday school mode. Jesus is for me and Jesus died for me! I couldn't fix my eyes on Jesus as the *perfector* of faith because I was too busy with me. I realized that I was emotionally stuck and I didn't know how to get myself out. In the past a way out was always made for me. In the past I had an option of another door and another choice. In that moment it became clear to me that I don't know how to fix this. And just maybe I should fix my eyes on Jesus. That was my hallelujah moment! I was still scared as hell but I didn't have any other option. I was scared to move forward but I was equally scared to stay where I was.

I remember thinking what else do I have to lose. I could feel the Holy Sprit overcoming me. Again my heart and head was fighting and I felt as if my soul was the prize. I realize how indecisive I was and how I had let fear paralyzed me. I wanted to be happy but I was afraid to choose happy. If happy was not what I thought it should be and what I perpetuated it to be then I am not choosing it! I feared the unknown. I had become my own worst enemy. I had to make a truce with myself and Hebrew 12 was my blueprint.

CHAPTER 5
FREE YOUR MIND THE REST WILL FOLLOW

" I am not what happen to me, I am what I choose to become." Carl Hauteur Jung

I'm not that chick…-Me

God and I were not at a happy medium. God and I were not of the same thought. I was still going through disappointment after disappointment. I was still in a job I hated with a passion. I was still hurt but healing from the past. My present day misery was like pulling scabs off of old wounds. I was trying my best to heal but it was slow moving.

I was still suffering from panic attacks. I had a bad breakdown after receiving some bad news. I was so overweight and I had fibroids. The doctor told me that I might not be able to have children. That news angered me and I blamed it on the stress of my job. When I told my grandmother she refuse to believe it. My grandmother became hysterical! She started crying, praying and screaming at the top of her voice!

She rejected the diagnosis. She refuses to believe it! She refuses to hear about my pain! I remember her saying that its impossible we are all fertile women! My granny kept saying, have faith, have faith. That was the one thing I was certain I did not have faith and oh yeah the ability to have a child.

With this news, my depression grew deeper. I was in so deep my emotions were sadness, anger and pain. I was faced with the reality that I have worked my ass off and I am sick as hell and can't enjoy the fruits of my labor. I was mad at God. No I was livid at God! I needed answers and I demanded answers from God. This was not cool. I had worked hard; I was a good girl I done everything right and I felt as if I was forgotten and abandon by God. I was not playing around with God any longer and I needed to know what's up why me what's going on? I begin to pray and listen and that small voice took me to Jeremiah 29; 11-14, *For I know the plans I have for you, declared the Lord plans to prosper you and not to harm you and plans to give you hope and a future. You will seek me and find me when you seek me with all your heart. I will be found by you declares the Lord, and will bring you back from captivity. I will gather you from all the nations and places where I have banished you, declares the Lord, and will bring you back to the place from which I carried you into exile.*

My first thought was what the hell does this mean God? You will seek me and find me. What? I go to church every Sunday. I'm showing up! I'm always there! I tithe! I am active! Is this not enough? I was under the impression that I was giving my all, my heart, my time, and my soul! What more can I give? In my anger I heard the small voice say to me, your worries, your sadness, your procrastination, and especially your lack of faith. I told myself that I don't have a problem with these things. I'm good as long as I am not at work. I was happy 70% of the time. The voice said I want 100% and more happiness for you child! I surrendered my anger in that moment and yield myself to the voice. I seek to understand what was important for my relationship with God. What does God want for me? What was I bringing or not bringing to the relationship? I had taught myself how to go through the motions and show up but I never participated. I had to seek to understand because my way and god's way was not the same.

I begin to look up banishment, exile and captivity. I prayed for understanding and clarity. I had to make it a point to build my faith. I had to make a point to affirm my faith. I had become a disgruntle employee being held captive by my lack of faith. But I didn't want that life. So I tried everyday to build my self-esteem and faith up. Some days were good and some days were bad! Some days I was strong and some days I was weak. But I wanted consistency. God was giving me consistency in our relationship but I was frustrated.

I tried talking to my friends and family but my pain fell on deaf ears. My friends were just tired of me because I blamed everyone for the situation and the racism that I faced. I always talk of change but I did nothing to change my attitude or behavior. It was humiliating to have a white man in management tell me to my face that I should be glad I am here. It's hard to go back to a job everyday when you know there are people there who are out to sabotage you! When you know that there are people who hate you for no reason! I would talk to my family and they would tell me I was stupid for wanting to leave that good job. It's hard when you're the first in your family to make it up, because people want to see you stay up there for their own reasons. There is no concern for the emotional damage that might be going on inside your head.

Family is the people who you think has your back. That was not true in my case. I love my family and I know they love me but people stay in situations for whatever reasons. I could no longer stay. I didn't want to compromise my health and my livelihood. I viewed my life as a contradiction of what God had promise me. But that was an error on my part. I simply did not understand the relationship I was in with God.

When the Vice President's next-door neighbor got the job, the person was right out of college; no degree in the field and had no experience. This validated two points for me. It's not what you know but it's whom you know and nepotism is just as strong as racism. This was another setback for me. I went home that night and laid in my tears of misery. My health was vanishing quickly. I started taking Vicodin to help me sleep but as my stress progressed I started using the Vicodin to get through the day. At night I would drink an entire bottle of Merlot to come down and watch episodes of HBO's The Corner. There were days I would not eat. I would only take pills and drink wine. My weight was fluctuating and I started to have massive chest pains. One night during my ritual of self pity. I heard the voice. This was my first divine encounter with the Holy Spirit. As I lay helpless in my bed the voice was as clear, firm and strong. I could not see anyone but I heard the voice. The voice said, no more. Not another drink or pill. The next morning was Sunday. I went to service and P.A. preached from Matthew 16, 24:26, " *if anyone would come after me they must deny themselves and take up their cross and follow me. For whoever wants to save their life will lose it but whoever loses their life for me will find it. What good will it be for a person if they gain the whole world, yet forfeits their soul? Or what can a person gives in exchange for the soul.* It was another riddle to me but at the end of the sermon P.A. explained that this sermon was not to win souls but to renew believers' faith. This message stayed on my heart.

The next day I took a fast and prayed for God to clear my mind. I prayed for understanding, trust and courage. I now wanted to know what was God's will for my life. I asked God to rid me of bad behaviors, thoughts, actions, people and influences in my life. I call this point in my life my death walk. I was dying to myself (the old Brenda) and now living for God. I cried because this meant letting go of everything that I wanted and hoped for. The next day I lost every person who I thought was a friend. People were dropping left and right even family members. It was an extreme clean up because I needed an extreme makeover in every area of my life.

I then asked God the big question, what is your will for my life. God replied, 'to write.' I was silent for a long time. God I went to school for automotive, I love cars. I don't have a degree in journalism or creative writing. I told God that I went to school for 5 years for this bachelor degree and it has to be put to some use. God replied I know how long you were in school. I was there. I want you to write. I always wanted to write but never entertained it because I didn't think I would benefit from it financially. The next day I had to take a fast for my mind. This was deep! I had to free my mind in order to live free!

The following summer I was back home in Chicago for the Black Expo and the Tate brothers, Larenz, Lahmard, and Larron, were there. They were talking about the lack of black writers in Hollywood. My assignment was coming up again from 3 actor brothers from the west side of Chicago. I met Bishop Vashti McKenzie and her words of advice for me were simply, "writers write!" I met E. Lynn Harris that year at an event in Detroit. I shared my desire to write with him. He was so excited and encouraged me to pursue it. I joked and said that John Singleton had done my story and he replied, it doesn't matter a story can be told many different ways. Just do it. I also met Susan Taylor her column in Essence Magazine was a monthly comfort to me. She encouraged me to pursue that which God has put out into the universe for me. I had my great cloud of witnesses cheering me on.

CHAPTER 6
ALL THINGS!

"Not everything that is faced can be changed. But nothing can be changed until it is faced." James Baldwin

Face the pain... -Me

In July of 1999, I was in the airport waiting on a delayed flight to take me home. I was flying to Chicago and then on to Ohio for a family reunion. I was in the airport crying because I felt like a loser. A guy who I had been dating and who I really liked broke up with me because he said I was too complicated. What does that even mean? I was hurt, confused, angry and depressed.

After about a 3-hour delay with my flight I conjured up the energy to walk over to the counter to check on the delay. The woman at the counter was very pleasant to me even though it was hard for me to keep my patience in check. She gave me a warm look over and said that she would upgrade me to first class. I didn't give a damn about first class I just wanted to get to my destination. I was surprise at the offer because I purchased the ticket for dirt-cheap so good for me! But little did I know God was up to something.

Once the plane had arrived, I boarded and took my place in first class along with the other businessmen. In that moment I didn't feel out of place because I have always been in the company of corporate men. In this moment I just wanted to relax in silence and in peace with my counterparts.

I settled into my big cozy seat and made eye contact with the men who stared at me probably wondering why I was in first class, I enjoyed the liquor that I should have said no to. I ate all the snacks that were offered to me. I wanted to enjoy the first class treatment. I just wanted to fly above the clouds in peace. Until...

One of the male flight attendants handed me a folded sheet of paper. I first saw numbers on the paper and assumed that it was a phone number. My anger began to rise. I thought the flight attendant was trying to pick me up or passing a note from someone else trying to come on to me. But that was not the case. Silly me it was another divine encounter.

Written on the paper was Romans 8:28. I could not believe it. This was what the flight attendant was giving me. A bible scripture. Romans 8:28 reads, *"and we know that in all things God works for the good of those who love him, who have been called according to his purpose. For those God foreknew he also predestined to be conformed to the likeness of his son, that he might be the firstborn among many brothers, And those he predestined, he also called and those he called he also justified, those he justified he also glorified, What then shall we say in response to this? If God is for us, who can be against us? He who did not spare his own son, but gave him up for us all, how will he not also along with him, graciously give us all things? Who will bring any charges against these whom God has chosen, it is God who justified, Who is he that condemns' Christ Jesus, who died more than that, who was raised into life is at the right hand of God and is interceding for us. Who shall separate us from the love of Christ? Shall trouble or hardship or persecution or famine or nakedness or danger or sword? As it is written for your sake, we face death all day long, we are considered as sheep to be slaughtered. No, in all these things we are more than conquerors through him who loved us. For I am convinced that neither death nor life, neither angels nor demons, neither the present nor the future, nor any power, neither height nor depth, nor anything else in all creation, will be able to separate us from the love of God that is in Christ Jesus our Lord."*

As I looked out of the window I could see dusk. I could see heaven as the sun went down and night appeared over the clouds and I heard a voice saying you are mine. I have called you by name and I will be with you always. You have nothing to fear. I felt so much comfort and peace in that moment. As I departed the plane the flight attendant took my hand and told me that God loves me and God will bless me.

The following Sunday my family worshiped together at the reunion. The sermon was Romans 8:28. All things in life need to be faced. But we need the courage of God to face all things. It took 80,000 feet in the sky and a total stranger for me to surrender my things to God! I was literally helpless during the flight. But God is always in control of all things.

CHAPTER 7
YOU PLAYED ME, NO YOU PLAYED YOURSELF!

If you want a good life, you have to do the work and let go-
Alfre Woodard

Trust God for the life you want…how can you trust God
when you don't even trust yourself? -Me

Sundays have always been my favorite day of the week. Its renewal day! Sunday gets you started for the workweek! I was standing on my balcony one Sunday afternoon, just looking up at heaven hoping I could catch a glimpse of something. I was still on my job from hell but my spirits were better. I was reading my bible and building my relationship and faith in God.

In studying, I found myself at the book of Matthew chapter 15. It was the story of the faith of the Canaanite Woman. *It's reads, leaving that place; Jesus withdrew to the region of Tyre and Sidon. A Canaanite woman from that vicinity came to him crying out, "Lord son of David, have mercy on me! My daughter is suffering terribly from demon*-possession." *Jesus did not answer a word; so his disciples came to him and urged him, "send her away, for she keeps crying out after us. He answered, I was sent only for the lost sheep of Israel." The woman came and knelt before him, "Lord, help me! She said, he replied, "It is not right to take the children's bread and toss it to the dogs." "Yes, Lord, she said, "but even the dogs eat the crumbs that fall from their master's table." Then Jesus answered, "Woman, you have great faith! Your request is granted." And her daughter was healed from that very hour.*

Well I am not going to lie. Again I was pissed! This Canaanite Woman was getting a blessing. Lord, I thought to myself she is taking my bread and I'm getting the crumbs. God you know that I am suffering. I am sick, I am miserable. I am lonely and you tell me this story about a woman who does not even believe in you but I am doing everything under the sun to please you.

God replied, wait a minute Brenda, the Canaanite woman has something that you lack, what I replied angrily! I love you, I follow you, I believe in you. God's reply was simply, you don't have faith in me. The Canaanite woman had faith even though I was not her God. She had faith in me and that is why I blessed her.

That reply messed me up! I felt so low and stupid. People who didn't even follow Jesus knew of his power and for that he blessed them. This was another pivotal turning point in my life. I begin to question my motives and what I really believed. I questioned my maturity and just how serious I was about my faith and being a follower of Jesus. I begin to take it seriously on what it meant for both God and myself. I realized that my habits and behaviors would be my demise. I knew it was something bigger than me, something more powerful than me, that simply wanted me to believe and with that belief to trust.

I had just been read, checked and treated by God. I could no longer treat God like a human. I could no longer expect human results from a divine being. In my stupidity and ignorance I realized that I was just playing myself. I don't even trust myself to trust God!

CHAPTER 8
I CAN'T BE PREGNANT!

Behold, I am doing a new thing. Now it springs forth do you not perceive it? - God

The more I got into the business of trusting God the better I begin to feel. It took baby steps. I would find myself comparing the relationship to past relationships of disappointments. So I worked hard not to let the work situation get the best of me.

I absorbed myself into my church home. I love Hartford Memorial Church. I was learning and growing and even giving some thought to serving on the deacon board. I heard that voice telling me to inquire but I was still bound by my past. I grew up very Baptist where I was told from the men and women in my family that women could not serve in the ministry.

It's funny because everything my family told me I couldn't do, God told me the opposite. I listen to my family but I was unhappy with my life. I listen to God things sound impossible but God said trust. I started to inquire about the deacon ministry. The men in my family were totally against women in ministry. Even some of the women in my family were against it. They talked about me and ridiculed my calling. That's a hurtful place to be when you're a young black woman alone in the world because where is your family? Where is your support system? Where are the people who say they love you? I had to really start to crawl out of that hurt and figure things out!

I would pray and study my bible and God always brought me back to Isaiah 66:9, *"do I bring to the moment of birth and not give delivery? Do I close up the womb when I bring to delivery?* I was pregnant with possibilities. I was horrified of what would become of me because I couldn't see it in my mind. I knew that God was calling me to ministry but I did not know what it looked like. I didn't have a vision for it. I'm pregnant with all these ideas and hopes for ministry but what will it mean for me and to others? God would never elaborate! God would say trust me and I will bring others to you to help you. I was scared as hell because I didn't have any fruit and I didn't know how to build God's kingdom! All I kept thinking was "Lord we in trouble."

CHAPTER 9
PICK UP YOUR MAT AND WALK!

"For every path you choose, there is another you must abandon usually forever." Joan D. Vinge

On December 28, 1999, I was in bed praying. The New Year was upon us and it was a special one. It was the next millennium. There was mass panic going on in the streets. People were talking like the end of the world was coming! But I did not care because God had promises for me! I knew God wouldn't let it end like that for me. I told God that I was not going to pray because God knows my prayers. However, I did say I want things to be different in 2000. The following morning I prayed and thanked God for another new day. God led me to Deuteronomy 2. It reads: *"then we turned back and set out towards the desert along the hill country of Seri. The Lord said to me, you have made your way around this hill country long enough, now turn north. Give the people these orders. You are about to pass through the territory of your brothers the descendants of Esau, who lives in Seri.*

They will be afraid of you, but be very careful. Do not provoke them to war for I will not give you any of their land, not even enough to put your foot on. I have given Esau the hill country of Seri as his own. You are to pay them for the food you eat and the water you drink. The lord your God has blessed you in all the works of your hands. He has watched over your journey through this vast desert. These forty years the lord your God has been with you and you have not lacked anything. Wow! This was so very true! I have been incredibly blessed. I have always had food in my stomach and shoes on my feet. The truth was right in front of me and I just have to believe it! I had been wandering in the desert long enough. It was time for me to go back home to my family.

I was excited about returning home! I didn't have a job offer. I didn't have a lot of money saved. I didn't have a place to live. I didn't know how I would do it. I did have that renewed sense of faith. I heard the small voice and everything in my being felt that it was correct. It was time to leave.

I never thought about what I was giving up. I never thought about what I was leaving. I had endured so much on my job it had no longer mattered to me. I was at peace with it! I was ecstatic that I had finally got directions from God. I was happy that God was finally moving. I didn't have the necessary means to move but I had something that I lost a long time ago. I had my faith back. I believed in God's plan that didn't include a lifeboat. God had become my lifeguard. After seven years of nothing but constant worry I was listening with my heart and ready to move forward. I can't swim but I knew that God would not let me drown.

God gave me my instructions and the time that I should leave. I would repeat this line everyday I felt fear creep in. My co-worker would always say this: For every step I take the Lord takes two! I begin to speak my words to keep me strong.

The next year I went back to work revived and refresh. I was scared but God said it would be done. I didn't tell anyone until the appropriate time. I knew from experience that if the wrong people found out they would have a field day. The ones that gave me the most problems were my family. They made fun of me for leaving such a good job. I was always the butt of the joke. These were the people who said they loved me but these were also the people who didn't have my best interest at heart. They are the people in my family who didn't want me to leave that job and who didn't want me in the ministry. Lines were being drawn because now I have to choose, what my family thinks or the way God makes me feel. It was a classic heart and head situation. It was complicated to say the least. I was leaving a well paying job and flirting with ministry. God had me looking so crazy! Or so I thought!

I started to pack up my home, pay off bills, and get things in order. I ended some relationships and I mended others. I cried all the time, tears of joy and tears of lost. I met some great people I was leaving behind and a great church. I had learned so much about ministry and being a part of a community of faith where women are welcome. I didn't know of other churches like this in Chicago and I could only wonder if they really existed. For me that church relationship was very important. I needed a good bible based church were I could continue to learn and grow. I needed to be around people who would build me up and not tear me down.

I worried about going back home and telling my family about my church and all that I have learned. That was a big concern for me. In prayer I told God my concerns and before I could utter the next word, God spoke to me and said, do you want to be healed? God knows my answer but before I could fix my mouth to speak. God said, pick up your mat and walk!

CHAPTER 10
WHERE TO WORSHIP? WHAT TO DO?

Change is always coming, be ready to act! - Me

After all of the confirmations from the Lord I was faced with the task of finding a place to worship. It was important to God that I find this new home before I made the move home. Once I was home I had to join that church. God didn't allow me any breaks I had to keep at it, building my faith.

PA and Hartford church was everything! I had never been so passionate about church before. So I had to find a new home that was just as powerful.

The Rev. Dr. Jeremiah Wright would preach the revivals at Hartford. I had heard of Rev. Wright from Chicago. He was the pastor on the Southside who put up the Free South Africa Sign! I remember seeing the sign while I was riding the 95th street bus! I also remember when Trinity United Church of Christ was being built. My thoughts were the skating rink is gone to build a church! (If I only knew then what was waiting for me at 400 W. 95th street)

I approached PA after a worship service and told him that I was moving back to Chicago and asked him for a suggestion for a church in Chicago. Without hesitation he said Trinity! I then went to God in prayer and asked. God said Trinity! Of course I had to challenge it and say that they are not Baptist. I then said I don't know anything about the United Church of Christ. I'd never heard of them. I told God that Rev. Wright is great, extremely intelligent and knowledgeable in all things but the church was not Baptist, how would this fit with my development? But God!! Now let me explain I felt that if God wanted me at Trinity UCC I would have been there years ago. Why would it take me to leave the city and come back to a church that was not on my side of town? I was raised in Chicago, if it was to be so, it would have happen a long time ago! It didn't make sense! God never makes sense.

In my mind if I would join Trinity that would be compromising my faith. I didn't want my sobriety to be compromised. Later that night I prayed and God led me to Jeremiah 3:15 which reads, *I will give you a shepherd after my own heart who will lead you with knowledge and understanding,* The Lord broke it down for me. PA and Hartford's purpose was to help me restore my faith. PA is a scholar and his purpose is to teach me about God's power and love. So I can build a relationship with God on faith and to know that there is nothing I can do without God. Rev. Wright is a scholar as well but will teach you what it means to be black and a Christian. Rev. Wright will teach you about our culture and how your womanhood is important to the body of Christ. He will teach you what it means to be a black woman in white America. He will teach you how to be worthy even when your self-esteem is gone! He will teach you about your ancestors. Most importantly he will prepare you to work for me!

I had accepted all of these lies. I believed every negative thing that was told to me by man. I believed that women could not be in ministry. I believed that I was not good enough. I stop fighting when things got hard and I just gave up. I floated in my tears and depression became my bed. I never thought I would be able to come back but with God...I did come back.

During the spring of 2000 I would make trips

back to Chicago to visit Trinity and get acquainted with the congregation and church functions. I went to the 7:30 service and stayed for the second and third service. I just didn't want to leave. I was so wrapped up in the spirit. I felt that if I left I would miss something. And I didn't want to miss a thing. I walked all over the church. In the fellowship hall there was a picture of Jeremiah Wright and the scripture was Jeremiah 3:15, a shepherd after my own heart. WOW! As usual God was right! It was my visual confirmation that I was in the right house. I was where God wanted me to be. Trinity United Church of Christ has open so many doors of opportunities and opened my mind to new thinking and living. I was becoming a black woman with pride, faith, and courage. I was becoming the person God wanted me to be.

Chapter 11
Effective Immediately

"It takes a huge effort to free yourself from memory- Paulo Coelho

Healing is a long and sometime difficult process in which I am still working through. Life experiences will stick in the mind and burn the soul. I had to make major efforts to believe in the process that was set out for me by God.

I had to believe in myself. I had to believe in the promises that God has for me! I had to relearn trusting again. I had to trust myself! I didn't want to survive day from day. I wanted to live! I wanted to have a life I was proud of and enjoy. I had to be surrounded by people who shared my love for life. I had to be around lovers and not haters. I had to be around people who loved life and God. This meant refining my circle and my family. It meant cleaning up my house and getting things in order. I had to change everything about myself if I was going to give myself to God's will. I had to be open to new things, people and experiences. I had to release my anger and hurt. I had to let go! I had to be deliberate about doing things in a new way and not resorting back to the old way.

When it was time for me to leave my job my coworkers talked about me so bad! I was everything but a child of God. There were a few that supported my decision. I learned from that experience of leaving that courage is a great thing! It takes courage to walk away from a high paying job and leave a middle class life. My faith looked so foolish. I had nothing and was riding into the sunset on Interstate 94 heading to Chicago.

I returned to Chicago and even my family was mad and against my decision. But I had to trust what God told me and for once in my life God trumped what others thought of me. God was allowing me to just be and my family and friends were not. I was tired of explaining and defending my decisions on my call and to follow God! It was weird because I finally had the courage to just be me. It was just me with God and working through my mess, drama, disappointments and preparing myself for what God wanted me to do and not what others wanted me to do! This attitude was different and refreshing. I was finding myself and learning about me. In the past I never did that because I pleased people and not myself. I had to be selfish and please myself and take care of myself first before anyone else. I needed to be a best friend to Brenda!

For so long I was shame of myself because my life was not what I wanted it to be. My shame caused me to be depressed, confused and it messed up my self-esteem. It caused me to not hear God and to doubt the promises. I spend so much time thinking does God have any empathy for me? Does God see me? Will God help me? Everything God told me has happened. God would show up at the 11th hour and make everything new! God has proven God self to me so therefore I don't have to act with the behaviors of doubt, fear and anger any longer. I don't have to hold pain any longer.

My expectations and expectancies are changed for the better. I have to do the work on my end and know that God is holding me down on the other end. What God has done in the past, God will do again. I have to commit to trust and follow God. When I'm on that page with God it just feels right. It feels solid and I feel comfort. I'm not afraid and I'm not worried. I'm good! Perseverance has always been my strongest character. Now I have to use it for my faith. I have to persevere in my faith. I have to commit my happily ever after to God. So compromising for God is a good thing and contradicting my beliefs for God is even better thing. God gave us Jesus so we can live and live abundantly. Survival is so overrated. I don't want to survive I want to live! With that being said, I choose to believe!

CHAPTER 12
LORD I BELIEVE NOW WHAT?

"Learning the difference between disappointment and discouragement is knowing there might be pain involved but the pain should not cause me to lose hope." – Me

" You got me looking so crazy right now." –Beyoncé

I was unhappy with the outcome of what I expected for my career. I wanted one thing that I thought would make me whole. I overlooked the calling on my life because I let people, the people I loved tell me it couldn't be done or tell me to reach for something that they perceived as better. That's my disappointment. When my life didn't unfold the way I wanted it to it brought on my discouragement. I lost hope and all confidence in anything I had to offer the world.

My perseverance never allowed me to just stop. The sacrifices of my ancestors never allowed me to stop. The Holy Spirit never stops speaking to my heart, speaking to my mind or giving me encouragement to make it through another day.

When I loss all faith God never loss faith in me. That's a wow moment! When you know that no matter what, I am in God's grip! God has made a covenant a promise for my life. I belong to God and no one else. I am given to my parents as a child to love and raise up. I'm a sister, an aunt, a friend, and a relative, but to God, I am God's child. I am God's daughter. I am God's property. I belong to God and not to the world. Jesus death resolved everything for me. I don't have to worry, I don't have to be discourage or disappointed. Jesus took up my infirmities and my sorrows. Therefore all I had to do was follow my calling. Following my calling meant having crazy faith and I finally got it! I finally release the fear and recaptured my faith.

What I know from this journey is that faith is about belief. Belief is about faith. They go together. Faith is a constant that must be renewed. The call that God has on our lives must be encouraged all the time.

Faith is about trust and it's about courage. It's about letting God lead you even if you look foolish in the process. Even if the people you love tell you no. It's about not proceeding with caution but it's about no matter what, if I fall God is going to pick me up!

When I left my corporate job you would have thought I committed a crime. The people who say they love me ridicule me the most. I was talked about and laughed at. Leaving is up there with one of the best things I have ever done in my life. I am happy and I am at peace. I compare my emotions to James Cleveland's "Peace be still." That's where my heart is. I am at peace. The people that discouraged me God has moved them out of my life. They pop up every now and then but God will shut it down for you! Once you establish yourself in God, your peace and your faith will not be disrupted.

I am happy and healthy, I lost the weight and I am managing my stress. I have ended toxic relationships. I got my mind right and back on track. I am focus, I have forgiven, I am healing my wounds, I humbled myself, I trust my skills and abilities, I sought help. I put me first. I am optimistic, I am teachable, I have completed seminary, I am writing. I am preaching. I am healed. I am whole and I am well. I am telling everyone about the goodness and mercy of God. I am confident. Most importantly I am faithful. God is guiding me. I know I might look crazy and this book might sound crazy to some but this is a testimony of God's love and power. So your faith will not rest on what the world tells you that can't be done, but it rest in the sovereignty of God!

MY DISCLAIMER

"When I had nothing to lose, I had everything. When I stopped being who I am, I found myself." Paulo Coelho

I have a duty to speak the truth the way I experienced it. I have a duty to share my faith and how the little faith I had helped me to survive. Now I can celebrate my journey through the rain.

My thoughts, my opinions, my fears, my courage, my happiness, my insecurities, my joys, my regrets, my failures, my pain, my triumphs, my comebacks, my adventures, my money, my hustle, my highs, my lows, my faith, my sorrow, my mistakes, my disbelief, my journey, my hurts, my embarrassment, my growth, my story, my experiences, my time, my sacrifice, my development, my divine encounters, my God, my love, my pen, my mind, my heart, my salvation, my life. No filters, no fillers just me! I give myself permission to just be me and celebrate all the good and bad that makes me, me.

When it comes down to it, it's all about us and what makes us happy, healthy, and productive, functional individuals. It's about the treatment we give to others and what we receive from others. We have to take care of ourselves first and let God take care of the rest. It's about the calling on our lives and what we do with that calling and how do we respond to that calling. It's about belief in faith. Its about believing in what our eyes can not see as of yet. I now can say proudly and with authority, Lord I believe!

ABOUT THE AUTHOR

Minister Brenda Summerville is a theologian, writer, activist and philanthropist. Brenda is a technologist by trade and has over 30 years of experience in Corporate America. She earned her Master of Divinity degree from Chicago Theological Seminary. Being an entrepreneur she focuses her expertise on corporate chaplaincy, womanist theology, pop culture and theology. Brenda also maintains a blog where pop culture and theology meets entitled: I'm not blogging I'm doing public theology.

Brenda is also the founder and director of The Summerville Kids; a non-profit organization that provides scholarships to high school seniors whose family have been affected by drug abuse. She has been featured twice in the online magazine, "The Girls Guide to Swagger," where she showcased her spiritual swagger. Brenda is an ordained Deacon at Trinity United Church of Christ and has started the ordination process with The United Church of Christ. She is a champion for women and work to resolve poverty issues. The ambitious entrepreneur is currently working on a spirituality and lifestyle book. Brenda resides in Chicago where she is an avid reader, an aficionado of lipstick, enjoys health, fitness travel, and is a lover of wine.